A DAILY BOOK OF PAGAN PRAYER

2nd Edition

Expanded and Updated

Megan Day

DEDICATION

To all pagans everywhere.

A PAGAN PRAYER PER DAY

Every day, above us, the sun rises, everything on the earth responds to its light and warmth, and life surges from the roots up. We are immersed in it, but somehow feel apart from it – because for most of us, it is pavement beneath our feet and the rhythm of digital appliances that pound out the measure of our days.

The cycles of the sun and moon continue, as always, and we are disconnected from them. We strain to hear birdsong, we are blinded to the budding of leaves. Can we be too busy and far removed from our natural environment to be pagan? Can it be too hectic, too technical, to ever find a spiritual touchstone? Or can we can find five minutes in the morning and another five minutes at night to light a candle, focus on a grounding thought, and sense the timeless rhythms that surround us? Can we unplug, but reconnect?

It is my hope that this book will help to do just that.

The daily rituals in this book are simple. At the start of each day, or the end of each day, or both, light a candle. It can be any candle. Or it can be one that corresponds with the energy of the day. Not sure what that is? It is provided for you on each page.

Set up a space, or altar, as elaborate or as simple as you like. I collect seashells, bird feathers, pine cones, interesting rocks, and arrange them around my central candle. I have different altar cloths to match the day's energy. I also have a candelabra with candles to represent all of the elemental forms of energy – green for earth, blue for water, white for air, red for fire, silver for the moon, gold for the sun. But just a dish with a white candle will do as well. All of the externals are just that – outer representations of what is going on inside. And it is the inner work that counts.

1

So light the candle, calm your mind, read the text, and take it all in. Add talismans of your own, words of your own, connections of your own. Paganism is all about your individual connection to the framework of the universe. It is about how you align yourself with its energies and make them work for you.

This book is intended to be a jumping off point – a way to kickstart the process of reconnection, realignment, and rebirth. Take it wherever you want to go. In the light of the flickering flame, take some small steps to get back on the earthen path beneath our feet.

Megan

WHAT IS A PAGAN?
AND HOW DOES MAGICK WORK?

Everyone who becomes interested in this path asks the same questions. What does it mean to be pagan? What do pagans believe? What do pagans do? Is there a secret handshake?? (No!)

There are so many resources out there that it can, in fact, be confusing rather than helpful. So here it is in a nutshell (which seems appropriate).

Contemporary pagans are not direct descendants, in the spiritual sense, of ancient pagans. Too much of what they originally practiced is lost, or irrelevant, to us. Sure there are some folks out there who 'worship' Isis or Thor and come as close as they can to the original organization of those cults. But there are a lot of gaps that have to be filled in.

For the most part, pagans are those who have rejected the major religions of the world – the Judeo-Christian-Islamic forms. Generally, pagans are atheists. Yes, some are polytheists – although I find that, as contradictory as it seems, this is still essentially atheistic. The pantheon of gods tend to be, much as the moon and sun are, representations of different aspects that make it easy to visualize and identify with certain forms of energy. Our brains like to use pictures!

The real crux of paganism is that there is no god outside of ourselves that has set up a rule book and then judges, rewards, or punishes us. There are, however, energies that are the fundamental underpinnings of our entire universe. And we can alter and affect our life experience in the way that we align – or misalign – with those energies. And that is what we call magick.

Spells and rituals are outer manifestations of the inner work we do to align ourselves with the constant flux of energy that is the substrate of every material thing in our existence – from planets to subatomic particles. There is no real substance to anything without the underlying quantum interactions.

The sun, the moon, the planets, the constellations, the four directions, the four 'elements' (air, earth, fire, and water) are all images that we use to represent the basic aspects of these energies. Your mind is the most complex and remarkable quantum machine in existence and it can use these representations to do amazing things.

Every pagan tends to have their own beliefs, so don't expect a bible. And don't expect two pagans to agree on every aspect of paganism.

Just explore and search and learn and take what is useful, discard what is not. The important thing is to know that there is no sin, there is no devil, there is no one to tell you what to do except YOU.

The basic tenet, and only 'commandment' that we need is the pagan precept: Harm none.

Do what you will, but harm NONE. That includes yourself. If every action, every thought, every intention is guided by this precept, then your actions do need to be dictated by a rule book.

This ties in with what we do when we perform magick. I know everyone wants to become a witch or warlock or wizard right away and make it rain or give your enemies warts. But that is fantasy. What we really do with magick is more straightforward. And it works.

We are immersed in a miasma of competing energies. Every being on the planet has wants, needs, desires, and impulses. It is a full time job just to identify, solidify, and implement our own goals and desires, let alone influence someone else's.

So the idea of using magick to change someone's else's behavior or circumstances or the behavior of nature is not realistic. Or achievable. What can you change? You.

You can align yourself with the energies that will help you 'vibrate', so to speak, in concordance with what you want. And knowing what you truly want can take a lifetime, so don't imagine that this means you light a candle and win the lottery.

What CAN we do with magick? We can protect ourselves. I can't force another person to do or not do something, but I can align energies to protect myself from what they do. We can attract things to ourselves. Attract people. Attract opportunities. Attract prosperity.

So paganism is about personal responsibility. We don't ask for some entity outside of ourselves to fix things. We spend some time and energy and use our ability to focus - and we fix things ourselves. And harm no one when we do so.

CORRESPONDENCES

Colors, elements, planets, directions – all of these are entities in the outer world that correspond with the fundamental energies at the basis of all existence. And it is those energies that we want to harness, or align with, in order to manifest our intentions. In other words, they are tools that help us with our magickal work.

That is why for every daily prayer in this book there is a corresponding color (for the candle), planet (associated with the day of the week), and element (associated with the planet and the day of the week).

Here is a brief summary of how these work.

COLORS AND ELEMENTS

The four elements are earth, fire, air, and water. These are clearly very basic representations of the fundamental types of energies. Each element has a color that is associated with it. These are very much tied in to the way our brains respond to color (and color is just light vibration). So these are a sort of signaling system for your brain to get it attuned to specific energies.

FIRE – is associated with the colors red, yellow, and orange. It is a fascinating element in that is the fiercest form of energy, both for destruction and creation. It is never passive, in either capacity.

EARTH – is associated with pink and greens and browns. It is a solid energy, a foundation. It can withstand a tremendous amount of pressure but can also shake violently. And crack. It is the perfect energy for resilience.

AIR – is associated with white and silver. Air is the most nebulous of the energies, ranging from whisper soft to hurricane rage. It is a vital, ubiquitous element. Air changes things quickly.

WATER – is associated with blues and purples. It is an adaptable, moveable energy. Like all of the elements, it has two very different forms – placid and tsunami. Water also has an interesting aspect in that it can be beneath our feet, or it can fall from the sky. Water can wear things down – or wash them away.

PLANETS, GUIDES, AND THE DAYS OF THE WEEK

In this book, we focus on the planets associated with the days of the week. Each planet is associated with a deity in mythology – either Greek, Roman, Egyptian, or Norse, or combinations of these – and these deities can be useful visuals for the energies associated with each day. I think of them, and their counterparts in other cultures, as 'guides'.

SUN – I guess I have to state the obvious and say this is the celestial body (a star, not a planet) associated with Sunday. The Sun has been worshiped for as long as we know what people have worshiped. It didn't take folks long to figure out that it was the source of light, heat, and life. The sun is therefore associated with creative energy and with the element of fire. One of the best known sun deities is Ra, of ancient Egypt. But there are many, associated with many cultures.

MOON – Perhaps a tiny bit less obviously, this is the planetary object associated with Monday. The Moon has also been an object of worship throughout the existence of humans, often seen as a sibling or companion to the sun. The moon is especially fascinating because it visibly changes throughout the month, waxing and waning. It is perhaps because of its changeability that is associated with air. One of the best known moon deities is the Roman goddess Diana, the huntress. But there are many, associated with many cultures.

The phases of the moon are important to take into account with your magickal intentions. A waning moon is associated with pulling things away, the waxing moon is associated with attracting things.

MARS – is associated with Tuesday. In Nordic mythology, the equivalent of Mars was Tiw. With just binoculars, you can look at Mars in the night sky and see that it has a red hue. It is associated with action – not violence! We tend to think of Mars as the god of war, but he was, above all, a protector.

MERCURY – in Nordic mythology, Mercury the Messenger was represented by Woden. That's how we ended up with Wednesday (though he was also known as Odin). Famed as a 'messenger', Mercury also represented eloquence and poetry. For the Norse, Woden was the epitome of wisdom. Because of Mercury's 'mercurial' nature, it is associated with air and changeability.

JUPITER – again, we ended up with the Norse version, Thor, who got Thursday named after him. He is associated with thunder, and thus with storms and the sky and the weather in general. Therefore, he is strongly linked with water and the colors blue and purple.

EARTH – the Nordic goddess of the earth was Freya, and Friday was named for her. It is not difficult to see this association, the fecundity and nurturing of an earthy goddess is the perfect symbol of earth's abundance. This is a powerful combination of planet and element.

SATURN – no Nordic name change for this one. The very serious Saturn gives his name to one of our favorite, most fun days of the week (Saturday, if you didn't figure it out). Although associated with air, Saturn is also symbolized by the color black. This is because Saturn is associated with the Greek god, Chronos, and is therefore slightly tinged with the notion of chaos.

THE FOUR POINTS OF THE COMPASS

Although the directions are not specified in this book, it is a good idea to keep them in mind. The directions correlate with the elements, so you can tie the elements, colors, and planets all together. You may want to keep the direction you will be facing in mind when setting up your altar. Orienting yourself towards a specific direction can be a useful way to amplify your intended energy when you are working your magick.

EAST is associated with air.
SOUTH is associated with fire.
NORTH is associated with earth.
WEST is associated with water.

There is a myriad of other correspondences – herbs, incenses, astrological signs, etc. Explore them and add what works for you.

HOW TO USE THIS BOOK

There are 35 pages of daily prayers, for a total of five weeks. Start on the day of the week at any number you want, and rotate your way through. In this way, you do not have the same text for say, the first Monday of every month.

Light a candle of the color that corresponds, read the text, take a moment to contemplate. Or just light any old candle you have, or just look out of the window. Improvise! Adapt! Do whatever works best for you. There is also a prayer in the same theme to read at night.

At the end of the book are separate, longer texts for the eight sabbats of the pagan Wheel of the Year: Samhain (October 31), Yule (December 22), Imbolc (February 21), Ostara (March 21), Beltane (May 1), Midsummer (June 21), Lammas (August 1), and Mabon (September 21). Many of these have variable dates, so these are just guidelines.

This is a daily invocation I use every day as I light my candelabra. 'Mote it be' is real old school paganism. It's always good to remember our roots.

Powers that are
Powers that be
Powers of earth, air, fire, moon, sun, and sea
Protect, guide, and nurture
My loved ones and me
This is my will
So mote it be.

1 MONDAY

Color: Silver
Element: Air
Planet: Moon
Guide: Diana

Morning:

Today is a day to focus on the thoughts, ideas, and actions that contribute to my inner peace. I can deal with the winds of change only if I am at peace within myself. Today I banish all thoughts and actions that create disharmony. I am calm, physically and emotionally. Today, I radiate peace.

Evening:

I know that I did my best today to focus on peace and calm. Tonight I rest knowing that my mind and spirit are peaceful. I can rest with a peaceful mind and face a new day tomorrow.

2 TUESDAY

Color:	Red
Element:	Fire
Planet:	Mars
Guide:	Mars

Morning:

Today is a day to focus on the strength that I must have in order to do what I need to do. There are many kinds of strength – strength of character, the strength of my body, the strength of my beliefs. I can be called on at any time to use one or all of them. I can be strong when I need to be, and use my strength to protect, to defend, to withstand. I can use all of my strengths today, wisely and meaningfully, as and when I need to.

Evening:

I know that I did my best today to focus on strength in all its forms. Tonight I rest knowing that when I needed to, I did my utmost to use my strength of body, mind, and spirit.

3 WEDNESDAY

Color:	White
Element:	Air
Planet:	Mercury
Guide:	Mercury

Morning:

Today is a day to focus on success. There may be tangible things I want to achieve, specific tokens of achievement that I aim for. But I will also remember that success is measured in many ways. As I move forward towards my goals, I will not measure my success based on what others judge to be successful, but only by my own inner guide.

Evening:

I know that I did my best today to focus on success, and that I am always successful in the ways that are most meaningful to me. Tonight I will rest knowing that the universe and all its energies supports my success, in all its forms.

4 THURSDAY

Color:	Purple
Element:	Water
Planet:	Jupiter
Guide:	Jupiter

Morning:

Today is a day to focus on creativity. I am both the product of a creative universe and a part of its ongoing creativity. Every day that I walk through this world is a day in which I create something just by being present. Creativity is my greatest power and I will use it consciously and carefully. Whatever good I want to see brought into the world, I can help create it today.

Evening:

I know that I did my best today to focus on creativity, and I can rest tonight knowing that I was part of the creative process of the universe. Even in my sleep, I continue to be a creative being.

5 FRIDAY

Color:	Pink
Element:	Earth
Planet:	Earth
Guide:	Freya

Morning:

Today is a day to focus on abundance – the abundance I already have in my life and the abundance I wish to create. As I look at the abundance of life on this earth, I know that I am at the center of a creative, evolving universe that will always provide abundantly. I immerse myself in the productive, fertile process of abundance in all of its aspects.

Evening:

I know that I did my best today to focus on abundance. I can rest tonight knowing that I am part of an abundant universe, and I cannot help but be a part of it.

6 SATURDAY

Color: Black
Element: Air
Planet: Saturn
Guide: Saturn

Morning:

Today is a day to focus on positivity. Positive energy attracts positive energy and repels negative energy. I can bring more positive things into my life by letting go of negative thoughts, beliefs, and attitudes about myself and others. I especially need to let go of negative thoughts and feelings about myself. I don't have to force anything – I just need to let them go.

Evening:

I know that I did my best today to focus on being positive in thought, word, and action. I can rest tonight knowing that good things can come into my life because I have the power to make them manifest..

7 SUNDAY

Color: Yellow
Element: Fire
Planet: Sun
Guide: Ra

Morning:

Today is a day to focus on feeling safe. I am surrounded by loved ones, I am a member of a community, and I am an inextricable part of the web of life. I am safe physically and emotionally, and stand in the light of the sun, not in the shadow.

Evening:

Tonight I will rest knowing that I will sleep safely, that my loved ones will sleep safely, and that it is the nature of the universe to nurture and protect.

8 MONDAY

Color: Silver
Element: Air
Planet: Moon
Guide: Thoth

Morning:

Today is a day to focus on words. The words I speak, the words I hear, the words I read. Words have power, and I need to be aware of that power. The energy that I put into my words can be creative or destructive. Today I will use my power to communicate wisely and I will focus on the good effect I can have with positive words and ideas.

Evening:

I know that what I did and said today made a difference. I will rest tonight knowing that I made an effort today to ensure that my thoughts and words had a positive effect on the world around me.

9 TUESDAY

Color:	Red
Element:	Fire
Planet:	Mars
Guide:	Tiw

Morning:

Today is a day to focus on bringing passion to everything I do. Not just the things that it is easy for me to feel passionate about – but everything I have to do. My intention today is to do everything with the energy, focus, and commitment that comes from true inner passion.

Evening:

I know that I did my best today to focus on infusing my life with passion. I know that I can live every day of my life with passion – the passion to love, to learn, and to contribute.

10 WEDNESDAY

Color: White
Element: Air
Planet: Mercury
Guide: Woden

Morning:

Today is a day to focus on justice. Justice, fairness, equity – all of these are aspects of the balance of the universe. I do not need to enforce justice, I do not need to decide what is just. I do not worry about what I think is unfair. I keep myself balanced and deal with everything and everyone around me in a just manner, and allow the energy of the universe to maintain balance.

Evening:

I know that I did my best today to focus on justice. Tonight I will rest knowing that I live in a universe that brings balance and harmony to all things.

11 THURSDAY

Color:	Blue
Element:	Water
Planet:	Jupiter
Guide:	Zeus

Morning:

Today is a day to focus on justice. Justice, fairness, equity – all of these are aspects of the balance of the universe. I do not need to enforce justice, I do not need to decide what is just. I do not worry about what I think is unfair. I keep myself balanced and deal with everything and everyone around me in a just manner, and allow the energy of the universe to maintain balance.

Evening:

I know that I did my best today to focus on justice. Tonight I will rest knowing that I live in a universe that brings balance and harmony to all things.

12 FRIDAY

Color: Green
Element: Earth
Planet: Earth
Guide: Gaia

Morning:

Today is a day to focus on growth. Every day is an opportunity for me to grow as a person, to grow in spirit, to grow in knowledge, to grow in understanding. There may be some limits to my physical growth, but there is no limit to how far I can expand my mind. Today I will look to each experience as a chance to grow – in mind, body, and spirit.

Evening:

I know that I did my best today to focus on growth and expansion. Tonight I will rest knowing that every moment of my existence – even when I sleep – is a moment in which my being can expand and grow..

13 SATURDAY

Color: Black
Element: Air
Planet: Saturn
Guide: Chronos

Morning:

Today is a day to focus on right action. Negative thoughts and feelings don't lead to right actions. I need to let those thoughts, feelings, and ideas go and make all of my thoughts right thoughts. Right thoughts lead to right actions. Right actions lead to good results. Today I welcome only good things into my life.

Evening:

I know that I did my best today to focus on right actions and positive thoughts. Tonight I will rest knowing that I filled my day with positive thoughts, positive feelings, and positive actions.

14 SUNDAY

Color: Gold
Element: Fire
Planet: Sun
Guide: Apollo

Morning:

Today is a day to focus on happiness. Happiness <u>for</u> me can only be defined <u>by</u> me. No one can tell me what will make me happy. I know that happiness does not come from the outer world, but is the deep contentment that comes from being at peace with myself. True happiness is not fleeting, but is deeply rooted. Today I will cherish my happiness and share it with everyone I can.

Evening:

I know that I did my best today to focus on happiness. Tonight I will rest knowing that I can be truly happy no matter what is going on in the outer world. And once I have happiness, no one can take it from me.

15 MONDAY

Color: Silver
Element: Air
Planet: Moon
Guide: Isis

Morning:

Today is a day to focus on being a spiritual being. I inhabit a physical body that moves through the world, but that is not my inner self, my true self, my timeless self. I will remove my attention, as much as I can, from the distractions of the outer world and concentrate on my spiritual being. And I will try to see the inner, true self of every other being I meet today.

Evening:

I know that I did my best today to focus on my spiritual self. Tonight I will rest knowing that I now have a better understanding of myself as a spiritual being, allowing the light and power of the universe to manifest through me.

16 TUESDAY

Color:	Orange
Element:	Fire
Planet:	Mars
Guide:	Bellona

Morning:

Today is a day to focus on courage. I have the courage to make the decisions that must be made, to do the work that must be done, to face the things that must be faced. I summon the courage of the warrior and protector and manifest it in my life. I acknowledge the courage within myself and also honor the courage I see in others.

Evening:

I know that I did my best today to focus on courage. Tonight I will rest knowing that I had the courage to get through another day. I faced the challenges, knowing that the infinite courage of the universe is there for me when I need it.

17 WEDNESDAY

Color: White
Element: Air
Planet: Mercury
Guide: Anansi

Morning:

Today is a day to focus on achievement. What are the things I want to achieve? Success? Fame? Fulfillment? Wealth? Peace? Forgiveness? Whatever I want to achieve, I can bring into my life now. I bring my thoughts into alignment with my intentions. And my actions into alignment with my thoughts. Today, my thoughts and actions will be directed towards my goals.

Evening:

I know that I did my best today to focus on achievement. Tonight I will rest knowing that I spent a productive day working towards my goals. Even if my achievements aren't evident to others, I know that I continue to make progress on both the material and spiritual levels.

18   THURSDAY

Color:	Purple
Element:	Water
Planet:	Jupiter
Guide:	Indra

Morning:

Today is a day to focus on serenity. I will remove those things from my life that are not contributing to my serenity and sense of calm. Actions, thoughts, habits, people, places, things – whatever does not contribute to my sense of calm and balance will be replaced with actions, thoughts, habits, people, places, and things that keep me poised and calm and serene.

Evening:

I know that I did my best today to focus on staying calm and serene. Tonight I will rest knowing that I can sleep serenely. Those things in my life that were keeping me unbalances have no power over me and I am serene, calm, and tranquil.

19 FRIDAY

Color: Brown
Element: Earth
Planet: Earth
Guide: Danu

Morning:

Today is a day to focus on nurturing. I can nurture the people and other beings around me that need to be nurtured. Nurturing can be physical, by helping with material needs for sustenance or growth. Or it can be emotional, showing love, attention, and respect. Today I will look for ways to nurture my friends, my family, and my environment with my thoughts, my words, and my actions.

Evening:

I know that I did my best today to focus on nurturing those around me. Tonight I will rest knowing that contributed to the abundance of the universe by my actions as a nurturing being.

20 SATURDAY

Color:	**Black**
Element:	Air
Planet:	Saturn
Guide:	Ishtar

Morning:

Today is a day to focus on protection. I will protect my heart and mind from the negative thoughts, feelings, and actions of others. I do not immerse myself in problems. I do not worry about things I cannot control. I do not try to change people or things just because I think they should be different. Instead, I focus on the positive aspects of all people and situations.

Evening:

I know that I did my best today to focus on protecting myself. Tonight I will rest knowing that I kept a positive attitude by choosing to focus on the positive aspects of existence.

21 SUNDAY

Color: Yellow
Element: Fire
Planet: Sun
Guide: Belenos

Morning:

Today is a day to focus on humor. It is important to see the 'light' – as in the light side of things. Nothing unites me with other people more than laughter, and very few things are better for my health and peace of mind. Today I banish all thoughts that make me sad and welcome only those that make me, and everyone around me, smile.

Evening:

I know that I did my best today to focus on smiling and laughing. A smile on the outside cannot help but translate as a smile on the inside. And vice versa. Tonight I will rest knowing that I shared as many smiles as I could.

22 MONDAY

Color:	White
Element:	Air
Planet:	Moon
Guide:	Khonsu

Morning:

Today is a day to focus on my home. What does it mean to have a home? Is it a particular building? A specific set of rooms? Or is it the time when I feel safe, secure, and loved? If it is, then my home can be anywhere. And I can always make others feel that they too are home by sharing those feelings of well-being.

Evening:

I know that I did my best today to focus on my sense of feeling at home. Tonight I will rest knowing that wherever I am, I have a safe, secure, and loving home.

23 TUESDAY

Color: Red
Element: Fire
Planet: Mars
Guide: Minerva

Morning:

Today is a day to focus on energy. Energy can be removed, and I am going to take the energy out of the things I don't want in my life. No energy will go into negative thoughts about myself or others. No energy will go into actions that do not make my environment a better place. All of my energy will be focused on the places, thoughts, and beings that I want in my life. All others will be banished.

Evening:

I know that I did my best today to focus on energy and how to use it. Tonight I will rest knowing that negative thoughts and feelings have no energy in my life or in my being.

24 WEDNESDAY

Color: Silver
Element: Air
Planet: Mercury
Guide: Lugh

Morning:

Today is a day to focus on removing obstacles. Some days it feels like doors shut, roadblocks go up, stairs become steeper. Obstacles can teach me things, I know. But sometimes enough is enough and it is time to clear them out. Today I remove any obstacles of thought or action that are keeping me from reaching my goals. These obstacles will diminish and my way will be made clear.

Evening:

I know that I did my best today to focus on removing obstacles from my life's path. Tonight I will rest knowing that nothing prevents me from getting where I need to go and reaching my goals. Nothing can stop my intentions from manifesting.

25 THURSDAY

Color: Blue
Element: Water
Planet: Jupiter
Guide: Thunderbird

Morning:

Today is a day to focus on wisdom. Wisdom is not based on how smart I am, or how smart others think I am. Knowledge comes from the outside. Wisdom comes from within. I can be open to my experiences throughout the day and process them, evaluate them, add them to what I know. Synthesizing all of me experience adds to my wisdom. Today I will be open to this inner knowledge, and try to recognize it in others as well.

Evening:

I know that I did my best today to focus on wisdom. Tonight I will rest knowing that I am surrounded by wisdom, that I find it when I look within myself, and that I can also recognize it in others.

26 FRIDAY

Color: Pink
Element: Earth
Planet: Earth
Guide: Atum

Morning:

Today is a day to focus on healing. If my body needs healing, I attend to what I need to do physically. And I also heal my thoughts. I keep my thoughts and ideas positive, and let go of old hurts and ideas that have made me unhappy. I release those old ways of thinking and become a source of healing – for myself and others.

Evening:

I know that I did my best today to focus on healing. Tonight I will rest knowing that I have let go of unhappy thoughts, ideas, and grudges. I have filled my inner being with a sense of wholeness and completeness that I can share.

27 SATURDAY

Color: Black
Element: Air
Planet: Saturn
Guide: Fortuna

Morning:

Today is a day to focus on safety. I will remove from my mind any ideas that make think I am not safe. There are many beings and circumstances in the world that affect me and my surroundings. I cannot control them, but I can protect myself from them. I can deflect their negative energies and impulses. I am aware that I am protected by all of the forces of the universe and have no need to fear.

Evening:

I know that I did my best today to focus on feeling and staying safe. Tonight I will rest knowing that myself and my loved ones are always safe and protected, and that I will not give in to believing or feeling otherwise.

28 SUNDAY

Color: Gold
Element: Fire
Planet: Sun
Guide: Horus

Morning:

Today is a day to focus on wealth. Wealth can mean many things and can come in many forms. What would make me feel truly wealthy? Money? Acclaim? Possessions? Or am I confusing riches with wealth? Today I will bring into my life the unseen aspects of existence that truly make me wealthy – friendship, love, and peace.

Evening:

I know that I did my best today to focus on wealth. Tonight I will rest knowing that much of my wealth and prosperity cannot be seen by others – the wealth of loving and being loved, of being at peace within myself and sharing that peace with others.

29 MONDAY

Color: Silver
Element: Air
Planet: Moon
Guide: Artemis

Morning:

Today is a day to focus on my dreams. My dreams tell me a lot about myself. Each dream is a gift that can teach me about the inner workings of my mind, unobscured by real-world distractions. In my dreams, anything is possible. I will carry that dream-like sensibility into my life today and keep believing that there are no limits, no boundaries, no barriers. I will believe that dreams come true.

Evening:

I know that I did my best today to focus on my dreams. Tonight I will rest knowing that I can look forward to illuminating dreams – the kind I have in my sleep and the kind I carry in my heart.

30   TUESDAY

Color:	Red
Element:	Fire
Planet:	Mars
Guide:	The Morrigan

Morning:

Today is a day to focus on action. I have goals and dreams and now it is time to take action. I always continue the inner work of cultivating positive thought and ideas, but now it is time to also commit to performing actions, no matter how small, that will move me forward on my path towards making my dreams come true.

Evening:

I know that I did my best today to focus on taking action. Tonight I will rest knowing that I did things, said things, and accomplished things that bring me closer to reaching my goals..

31 WEDNESDAY

Color: White
Element: Air
Planet: Mercury
Guide: Brahma

Morning:

Today is a day to focus on ambition. What do I want to achieve? How far do I want to go? How high do I want to climb? What is keeping me from reaching the heights, from standing on the pinnacle? Today I will assess what I aim for and whether my aim is true. I have the tools to remove my obstacles, and achieve all things with good intention.

Evening:

I know that I did my best today to focus on my ambitions. Tonight I will rest knowing that I made progress towards achieving things that are important to me, whether they are big or small..

32 THURSDAY

Color:	Purple
Element:	Water
Planet:	Jupiter
Guide:	Shango

Morning:

Today is a day to focus on cleaning. Cleaning out the things I don't need. I will clean out and get rid of the negative feelings, regrets, grievances, grudges , and unhappy memories that clutter up my life. I no longer have room for these. I release them all, and I will spend the day with only good things, ideas, and thoughts that support me, in my heart and mind.

Evening:

I know that I did my best today to focus on cleaning out what I don't need. Tonight I will rest knowing that my heart and mind have released the debris of my old life, and made room for the new..

33 FRIDAY

Color: Green
Element: Earth
Planet: Earth
Guide: Ceres

Morning:

Today is a day to focus on attention. Sometimes life seems to go past me in a blur, days running into nights, nights running into days. I can slow life down just by paying attention to it. Today I will notice and be attentive to everything around me – people, places, things, animals, the weather. I will pay attention to what people say. I will pay attention to the color of the sky, the songs of the birds. I will pay attention to my own thoughts and words and ideas and remember to send positive ones into the universe so that they may be made manifest.

Evening:

I know that I did my best today to focus on being attentive. Tonight I will rest knowing that I paid attention to everyone around me and also my own inner thoughts. Through my attention I brought positive thoughts, ideas, actions, and energies into being.

34 SATURDAY

Color: Black
Element: Air
Planet: Saturn
Guide: Tyche

Morning:

Today is a day to focus on giving. The universe is a place of positive and negative, of push and pull, of give and take. I am a life-giving being. My awareness supports everything and everyone around me. Today I give energy to my positive thoughts and words. I give support to my harmonious relationships. I give attention and support to my environment. And above all, I give thanks for the gifts I have, the gifts I receive, and the gifts I share.

Evening:

I know that I did my best today to focus on giving. Tonight I will rest knowing that I make room for more gifts from the universe by giving and sharing.

35 SUNDAY

Color: Yellow
Element: Fire
Planet: Sun
Guide: Agni

Morning:

Today is a day to focus on balance. Sometimes my energy dips up or down, my mood swings, battles seem to be uphill, or opportunities seem to slide downhill. But these are outer appearances. Within myself, I am completely in balance. I am balanced physically through exercise and healthy food. I am balanced emotionally through loving, peaceful relationships. I am balanced mentally with happy, positive thoughts. From the inner to the outer, everything in my life today is in perfect balance.

Evening:

I know that I did my best today to focus on balance. Tonight I will rest knowing that I can achieve a healthy balance in all aspects of my life, including deep, restful sleep.

PAGAN WHEEL OF THE YEAR

Our ancestors were agrarian and the rhythms of the earth were critical for survival. The times to sow and plant, when to harvest, when to let the earth lay fallow, when to work, when to rest – these were all dictated by the moon and sun.

As much as Christianity has tried to overlay its precepts over the substrate of paganism, many of our major holidays still show their pagan roots. That is why so many of the eight 'sabbats', or festivals, in the pagan calendar will seem very familiar.

The wheel can be divided into quadrants – two sabbats in each of the four seasons of the northern hemisphere, the ones that most of us experience. The year for us begins at the end of October (Samhain), when the very last of the harvest had to be cleared from the field, followed by Yule – at the lowest point of the solar cycle, and then Imbolc, when the sun starts to return. In the spring, we have Ostara and Beltane, followed by Midsummer. On the first day of August is Lammas (or Lughnasa), then the autumn equinox at the end of September (Mabon). And so the wheel has turned. And we start again.

SAMHAIN (October 31)

In the dark folds of the chilly nights that fall earlier and earlier at this time of the year, the veil between the worlds of the living and dead is said to be at its thinnest. As the green leaves reach the end of their summer-long lives and mature into golds, crimsons, and browns, we can feel the earth settling down for its long winter nap, the deep roots of the trees nestling under the leaf blankets for a good long snooze. The end of the growing and harvest season was considered to be the end of the year by our farming ancestors. After all, the hard work was done. The coming winter was a time for rest and lots of sitting by the fire. The notion that winters were a time of hardship and privation is very false – after a good harvest in the fall, winter was not a time of scarcity. So as it was for our agricultural forebears, this time of year can be for us – a time of enjoying the fruits of out hard work and a time for contemplating the work to be done in the new year. But most especially, on those evenings when the veil slips to its sheerest and most transparent, it is a time to remember those who went before us, those upon whose shoulders we stand. Long ago the lighted jack-o-lanterns and scary masks were intended to ward away any wandering spirits who crossed over the veil who might not have been welcome. But at the same time, the sweets and parties and the fun and games were meant to make the cheery spirits welcome. This is still a good rule for the coming year – welcome in those who will guide and support you, and banish the old ghosts who only hinder you.

Samhain is usually pronounced 'sow-ann'.

YULE (December 21)

In the depths of the darkest heart of the long winter is one of our most joyous celebrations – a celebration of light, of warmth, and of joy. It is surely no coincidence that every culture in the northern hemisphere has a holiday at this time of year. Everyone who lives in this climate of darkening skies and days that have shortened and shortened until it would seem they might disappear altogether will know that the magick time when this deepening cycle ends, when the sun seems to turn around and wend its back into the wintry skies, is a time to be joyful. It is a time to celebrate the lengthening of the light that is making its return. This is also a good time to reflect on the fact that winter may seem like a dead time – a time when the flow of life freezes still and growth and productivity seem to stop altogether. But as anyone who has ever watched a spring unfold knows, beneath the cold cover of winter darkness, life is stirring and striving. We too must use this time to prepare ourselves so that when the longer golden days return, we are ready to blossom.

Yule is celebrated at the time of the winter solstice, so check your calendar and confirm the exact date. It varies from year to year but is generally between December 21 and 24.

IMBOLC (February 2)

The nights have been long, the darkness has been falling early – sometimes after a day that seemed to have barely crept into the short-lived light.. We know the days are actually getting longer, but the lengthening seems so small, the increments so undetectable. It is tempting to curl up and doze while waiting for a full-fledged spring. But the trees know better, the restless birds see the growing light, and the lambs are coming into the world on shaky legs that nonetheless find a sure footing. So we need to shake off our winter lethargy; it served us well as we stored up our energy during the dark and cold but it is now time to prepare for the growing season ahead. It is time to find our footing on the slippery grass of a new year and prepare ourselves for what we want to harvest in the coming months. Now we light our candles not to ward off the gloom, but to welcome even more light. And now we prepare the fields of our dreams and expectations for the sowing of our goals and ambitions. We prepare now for a glorious harvest to come.

Imbolc is the midpoint between the winter solstice and the spring equinox and is the first cross-quarter day of the year. The Christian church celebrates it as Candlemas.

OSTARA (March 22)

Even if spring is not fully sprung, it is hard not to feel full of anticipation at this time of year. Colorful eggs and chocolate bunnies, baby chicks and baskets of greenery, are all part of the upwelling of energy and enthusiasm that the burgeoning sunshine inspires. The increased sunlight and retreating cold creates a buzz that fills us with a sense of renewal. It is not surprising that this is a holy time of the year for everyone, across many faiths, as the radiance of the lengthening days can't help but draw us into the flow of growth and awakening that pulses in the roots and branches below and above us. As the tulips start to rear their heads, it is time for us also to rise out of our winter slumbers and prepare for a new season. We can plan our gardens. We can open our windows and let the breeze sweep away the winter dust. We can prepare for a new start, new chances, new experiences, because more than anything, spring is about being renewed. As the sun increases its long-reaching arc across the sky, we too must rise – and shine.

Ostara is named for Eostre, a Germanic goddess of the spring and the dawn. Yes, she was the one with the eggs and the bunnies. Unlike other holidays at this time of year, Ostara is not tied to the lunar calendar, but to the spring equinox. So check your calendar. It usually falls between the 20th and 25th of March.

BELTANE (May 1)

The warmth of the growing season is making itself felt now. Even the air seems pregnant with possibilities. Our hopes and plans should be well established in these longer days, but perhaps they are not full-fledged enough to escape the caprices of the winds of change or the rains of doubt that could threaten their tender roots. Join hands with those who are on the path with you. May Day has always been a time for people to come together and use the warm weather for two things – to protect what they have, and to ensure that their community maintains fertility and growth. Bonfires, flowers, and twirling around with ribbons were all part of banishing decay and stagnation. So dancing around the Maypole is all well and good – but be aware of when the time for dancing around an issue has ended.. And know when the time to light the fires of change has come.

It is believed that 'Beltane' is derived from a very old Celtic word for fire. As May Day, it is still a holiday in much of Europe.

MIDSUMMER (June 21)

Today is the longest day of the year, in some ways, the peak of the sun's power. Though it will be sunny for many more weeks, this is the point at which the days start to shorten. Slowly, slowly, the nights will lengthen. Soon it will be time to start harvesting from our gardens. But not quite yet. For now we still feel the heat in the air, still enjoy the long days that seem to trickle into late sunsets. This is a good time for us to think of our own peaks and valleys, our own highs and lows, to examine the light and dark of our own days. We remember all of the energy that it takes to bring the fullness of our lives to fruition. And we remember that as this energy begins to dim, as we start to relax and slow down just a bit, that we begin to see the results of what we started long ago, when the world was darker and colder. The peak of daylight is a time to celebrate light and warmth of the sun, and to remember that the wheel will turn full circle.

Midsummer is really the middle of the year, not the middle of the summer. It is the summer solstice, and generally occurs between June 20 to 25.

LAMMAS (August 1)

The first loaf of bread made from the first harvest of the year was called lammas bread, or a lammas loaf. For our ancestors who lived off of the land, late spring and early summer could be lean times. The stores from the previous harvest might be nearly used up and it was too early to harvest the next crop that had been planted in the spring. Many times there were very hungry people waiting for their lammas loaf in August. What do we hunger for? As we look past the summer that is now coming to a close and forward to an autumn harvest, what are we yearning for? What do we hope for? What do we dream of? What do we need, rather than merely want? At this time of the first harvest, we can take the measure of what we have been cultivating and pull the weeds that interfere with healthy growth. We can provide nourishment to the hopes, dreams, and goals that are yet to be harvested.

Lammas is sometimes called Lughnasa, after the Celtic god of light, Lugh. It is an agricultural celebration and not tied to the cycle of the sun.

MABON (September 21)

The wheel of the year is turning. The days have been slipping away ever so slowly since Midsummer and now the nights take over, creeping ever longer until the day dwindles into wintry shadows. Mabon is that half-way mark, the time when day and night are equals and neither can claim victory. But after today, that will change. The high heat of summer and the lazy days will truly be over. Do we fear the night or the darkness? Do we dread the lingering dusks of autumn and winter? It is our nature to crave light and warmth, after all. It is also our nature to need rest, to avert our eyes from the glare of intense radiance and to look inward on occasion. The earth cycles through intensities of light and dark, but only after teetering briefly on the brink of absolute symmetry. So too we have parts of our lives that need full light and illumination for growth and expansion. And also parts of our lives that flourish best within ourselves, kept safe from outside exposure and interference. Now is a time when we, like the earth and the sun, can embrace all of those aspects of ourselves and bring them into perfect balance.

Mabon is the autumn equinox. Please check your calendar – it generally occurs between September 20 and 25.

ABOUT THE AUTHOR

Megan Day lives and works in County Kildare, Ireland. She trained as a Druid more than 20 years ago, but has been hugging trees for much longer.

Printed in Great
Britain
by Amazon